# PHASES

By Tre Hands

Thank you to my always loving family—
THIS is for you.


~ Tre

# Preface
## A brief word about the poems...

Truthfully speaking, we all change over time. We laugh at our peaks and cry at our valleys, then look back at the journey that led to where we currently are. To be in the state of *Waxing* simply means to be working towards something. It means putting fear aside and trying to reach for something that, at first, seems so far out of reach it seems impossible. Taking a chance, though, is half the battle. Things that seem so far-fetched might be a little more attainable than we think.

Upon reaching our goal, we float in this air of perfection called the *Full Moon* phase. Here, whatever we've reached for, we finally have. Instead of looking out to the future, we try to make that moment last a lifetime. It is the moment when the moon is the most visible in the sky. Simply put, it's a time period we never want to pass because it's the one we've looked forward to for so long.

Sadly, time keeps moving. All too often, the taller we stand, the harder we fall back to reality. *Waning* is a symbol for disappearance, loss, and decay. Mistakes made often lead to the end of that previous state of perfection and achievement. As we see less and less of the moon each night, we see less and less light; thus, less can be perceived of a life that is becoming far too grim. We wonder if we will ever be whole again, or if we will be like shattered glass. All good things do somehow come to an end.

Finally, in these last moments, we look back on what

we had—on the mistakes made—and begin to question what we could have done better or differently. *New Moon* is not about accepting the moon, for it is no longer visible. It is about seeing this as a period of rebirth and resolution. We begin to see past and beyond ... accepting our mistakes for just that—mistakes. The ebb and flow of the moon, it comes and goes; much like our lives, it is filled with highs and lows. Just as the moon constantly goes through its phases, we continually go through ours.

# PHASES

# Waxing

Phase One

# What Am I to You?

I don't know what I am to you.
I don't know what we'll ever be.
But...

Emotionally, I seem to be a falling leaf off of you, my beautiful tree.
If you are the sun, then I am a sunflower.

I don't know how to say it.
I don't know what "it" even is.
But...

Truthfully, you run through my mind all day long, like a song I keep on repeat.
If you are the sky, then I am a cloud.

I don't know how I got lost.
I don't know if I'll ever be found.
But...

Hopefully, we are opposites like two magnets destined to attract.
If you are the wind, then I am the aroma carried by it.

There's a lot I don't know.
But...

I do know that you are,
The oxygen to my lungs,
The train to my tracks,
The purpose to my life.

So, the only question is, what am I to you?

# Hidden Sun

(A truth that is being largely covered up for the benefit of
whoever is hiding it)

But what am I hiding?
My true feelings of passion for you?
For a while, I believed this was my hidden sun.
Yet, this was only the cover up.
No different than a lie told by myself to soften the harsh blow of
the truth.

In the mirror, I stare beyond the surface of my eyes.
I journey into the depths of truth by penetrating through the walls
of lies and deceit.

Here, I found my hidden sun.

And I'm sorry that I'm not as great as I said I was,
I'm sorry that deep down, I'm really scared of love.

Scared that love will bring pain.
Scared you won't love me back.
Scared if you do, you'll eventually leave me.

But your heart is so warm—I might just have to take that chance.

# Comfort Zone

Standing in the comfort of the sand, I wonder...
What am I missing?
As you lie out of my reach,
Just beyond the sand are the waves.
What if I get there and they crash down on me?
If I call out to you, will you respond?
What if I can't find the right words to say?
When I open my mouth,
Will the words sit on the tip of my tongue?
As you ride the waves out to a new life,
I ponder what I am missing...
Afraid to leave the comfort of the sand.

# Trust Fall

Falling from the clouds,
Hoping to be caught by you.
Distressed as my speed
Increases and as the ground
Only gets closer.
What if these are my
Last few moments?
To leap with no
Idea of where I'll land.
I put it all out there.
Now I fall.
Hoping to be caught...
By you.

# Searching for the Words

The truth is
I can't speak to you.
As words swirl through my head,
My tongue won't allow them to fall from my lips.
One day, I hope to gain the strength.
One day, I just know it will all work out.

# Perception

Maybe I want you to look at me,
And see more than just the person who sits next to you.
Maybe I want you to look at me,
And see what you always desired in someone.

# Jumping from the Cliff

Fear stops a lot of dreams.
Putting oneself out there, hanging on a zip line with no safety net
in case you fall.
Of course, fear will be evident, especially if you've never done it
before.
Taking such a large risk, and being so uncertain of the outcome.
It's like jumping from a cliff hoping there's someone to catch you.

It takes a lot of courage to be vulnerable and actually give
someone your all.
To know that you can give it everything you have and still end up
short.
Rejection is the invisible wall we place in front of ourselves
whenever we attempt anything.
Maybe if we stop thinking and just jump, maybe, just maybe, we'll
find what we are looking for.

# Praying Hands

Feel my words as they reach out to you.
Let them glide over your body and caress you.
My hands glued together as I look to the heavens above.
Asking not for riches, but for you to return.

Please hear my words of truth.
I need you on this earth with me.
I hope you hear me as I weep over you, my lost friend.
Water-filled eyes...my hands together, I call out to you.
Hoping you hear me and my truth.

## Uncluttered Mind

Free your mind of all distractions,
And look me in my eye.
Don't you feel these feelings?
The feelings that belong to only you and I.

## Blueprint

My mind racing,
Calculating every possible outcome.
And when the time comes,
An unimaginable path will happen.
Will I freeze again?

## Attempt at Life

I'd rather crash and burn
Trying to soar with you
Than fly forever without
Ever being with you.

## Storm Inside

My thoughts are the storm I've been avoiding.
Facing them means fears must be fought.
It means pain might strike.
It means I may lose the battle.
But, I can't do anything, anymore.
After all, the only way out is through.

# Sleep Pt.1 Dream

Sometimes it feels like I am dreaming,
To be next to a person so amazing,
To have a heart in my hand,
To see your eyes light up so brightly,
To feel love with all of its might.

Tonight, tonight is the night.
As we hold hands and stare at the moon,
I sense the perfection in the air,
Everything seems to be falling into place,
I see tears of joy in your eyes,
Truly, there is nothing more one could want.

Hours pass by, in what feel like seconds.
Together, we admire the starry night sky.
As you stand in front of me,
I feel the love between us—so strong.
Contentment fills my mind,
For I want nothing more nor less from this very moment.

I hear loud beeping coming from the sky.
It shrieks so loudly, I can hardly think.
But I'm holding you, what more is there to think?
Why won't the screaming stop?
I shoot out of my bed,
Now realizing it was just my alarm clock.
For, it was all a dream,
But my feelings for you are so real.
I'm ready to take a chance.
So, again, I fall fast asleep.

# The Distance Between Us

Why do you feel so far away?
Giving up might be the only true defeat, but how is it that
The closer I try to get to you, the farther you seem to be?

You sit a mere five feet away from me, yet
Those five feet feel like you're halfway across the world.
Although we never touched, I can feel your heart bouncing
Like an eager child soon to get a new toy.

My heart beats only for you;
Every moment with you is a dream come true, and sadly
Every second without you is a nightmare.

If you were here beside me, I'd tell you the joy you bring to my
life.
I'd tell you I stare because I can't keep my eyes off of you.
I'd tell you that I can't stop thinking about you.
I'd tell you I only want to be around you.

I guess I'll just keep waiting for the stars to align,
Or perhaps I'll wait for the next blue moon.
No matter the timeline, my heart and yours belong together.
The only thing stopping them is,
*The Distance Between Us*.

# Wishing Upon a Star

I wonder if this distance is bringing us closer together.
So what if we are miles apart?
If you grow and I grow, are we not still together?
May our paths be like two trees whose branches intertwine.

I spoke to fate, and she's a mysterious lady.
She refused to convey whether our futures will ever be linked.
Sometimes I find myself wishing upon a star.
I wish for my future to envelope you in it.
I wonder if the stars ever gaze in our direction.
And wish upon the big blue orb in the sky.

Do stars wish upon us, the way we wish upon them?
Would a star wish for there to be less distance between it and
other stars?
Do they envy humans because, unlike them, we can be close to
the ones we love?
Do they weep when they realize their paths will never cross?
Upon a star I wish for the chance to be with you for a lifetime.
I don't want to be apart any longer.

## Lone Star

You and I, dear star, are one and the same.
Not a single cloud chose to join you up so high.
Not only that, but even the moon stayed hidden.
Not even your fellow stars wanted to shine with you tonight.
You are the lone child of this barren mother sky.
And I am the lone star of this empty field.

Dear star, you and I are too often alone.
Is this your way of giving me an opportunity you've never had?
I haven't a clue on what to do from here.
Guide me to the light of a heart I know not of.
We are the same.

# Sun and Sunflower

I'm in love with the Sun.
Should its brightness give
Us all the joy we need?
You are the center of my soul.
A beam of light in all life's bleakness.
Golden honey drips from your peak
Until it reaches your pitfall.
It was only a matter of time
'Til you and I collide.
We are two rays of light destined to intertwine.

## Out of the Blue

You reached out to me, and I'm forever grateful.
In your arms, I found warmth.
In your eyes, I found beauty.
In your heart, I found home.
Unexpectedly, you showed me your best,
And I promise to give you nothing less than mine.

# Your Song

How can a melody be so beautiful and so raw at the same time?
Had I not closed my eyes, tears would have fallen freely.
The words you strung together were woven perfectly like from a
seamstress.
You managed to touch my heart by showing me a portion of
yours.

I want to be on your wavelength.
We connect so much deeper than I ever could have imagined.
Let's not go another day without talking.
Let me hear your voice because I don't think you know how
powerful your words truly are.

# Can I Write You a Love Poem?

Bring me into the limelight of your life.
Let me speak on powers that a human should not bestow.
Can my eyes even comprehend the sight of the beauty before
me?
In your face, I cannot see the slightest imperfection.

Let my love cover your body like drapes over a window.
Should you feel alone, close your eyes and know that I am with
you.
Can I hold your hand as we walk along this beautiful beach?
I followed the path to your heart much like Dorothy did the yellow
brick road.

I'm standing at the gates of your emotions, hoping you give me
the key to unlocking them.
My dear, please wait on me, for I know you are a prisoner at the
apex of this castle.
I promise to shout your name from the heavens above and the
depths of the sea—please hear me.
I won't leave this world until I deliver my message to you titled:
My First Love Poem.

## Gift

If I could,
I would gift you a rainbow.
So even when it rains,
You have something to look forward to.

## Our Paths

Call it what you want
But this is no accident.
This is your path in life,
Becoming intertwined with mine.

## Excitement

I'm excited beyond belief.
I stand up tall, ready to see
All the greatness that lies in front of me.
Whatever comes, I won't bequeath.
I cannot wait; where do we go from here?

## Apart, but Together

I don't know where I am;
I don't know where we should be
Will we ever meet?
You are the sky
And I am the sea.

# Tomorrow

The day may come tomorrow
When today's effort won't be enough.
May we rise into new glory,
May our bodies never fall short.
Should the day ever come,
Do we dread it or approach it woefully?
Much like a land full of grasses that change
With every new season,
We are fickle in how we should view a day not yet born.
So here we are, thoughts naked and bare.
Uncertain on what our nexus holds.

# Unchartered Waters

Like a sailor who's never ventured these waters,
I've never been down this path before.
I truly fear the mystery of what's to come.

I fear my thoughts that may shape reality.
No map I have foretells the dangers ahead.
Perhaps no danger resides on this journey.
If it does, will I be prepared?

In way too deep to turn back.
As you call my name,
I put aside the fears growing inside me.
I'm choosing to focus on the beauty
That may come from the unknown.

# Fine Wine

Let my mistakes mold me into a better me.
Should I fall short, don't tear me down like a failed project.
When I trip, don't count me a burden and continue on life's
voyage without me.
If I should drop, don't leave me behind like a weight off your
shoulders.

Please, don't let the harshness of this world chop and break me.
Carry me on your shoulders and hold me high one more time.
For today I may be subpar, but in time,
I promise to age like fine wine.

## Anticipation

The hour is sailing
Towards us.
Each passing moment filled
With anticipation.
The winds align,
Screaming for a result we know nothing of.
The rope tethering us to reality
Has now pulled us together.
For in this hour,
Are we not exactly where we need to be?

## Dreamer

I'm a dreamer
And maybe that's a problem
In my head, we fly
And we never come down.

## Red

Red is the color of fire.
It's also the color of love.
Oh! How fire burns so hot,
But the desire burns so long.

## What We See

Do you see what I see?
When our eyes lock,
Can you peer into
My innermost thoughts?
And read them like a book?
Can you feel my
Beating heart calling out
For you to notice it?
Do you see everything we can be?

# Wonder-Filled Eyes

A ball of light,
In the night, so dark.
You're a hero,
In a land of only villains.
I live my whole life
Wanting to be with you.
I refuse to falter now.
You mean everything to me.
If I could,
I'd wrap my arms around you.
So tight, in fact, that "you and me"
Would become "we."

# Need You

What is this light?
Warmth?
Happiness?
Pleasure?
Like a bumblebee to a flower.
Or rain to the grass.
I need you more than you do I.

## River of my Thoughts

My mind is an ocean,
And you constantly travel the
Mighty river leading to it.

## Artist

Be the sculptor
To my marble personality.
See me as what I can be,
Not who I am.

## Clouds Above

Are the clouds above friends?
Do they ever become acquainted?
I wonder if we'll ever be close
Like clouds when they join together.
Instead of being two, can we be one?

## Purpose

There I was, grasping at straws.
Questioning my very existence.
Along came you.
And with you, came my purpose.

# Better for You

You inspire me.
Do you ever think of that?
You give me a reason to rise.
I can't imagine being without you.
This feeling in my heart,
Is the feeling I never want to lose.
You shocked me,
And I hope to show you my newfound power.

# Mindset of Connection

The question is not would I die for you;
The question is would I live for you.
Would I strive every day for you?
Would I fight every night for you?
Would I spend every breathing moment
Of my day thinking of you?
You see, death is easy.
Anybody can die for anyone.
But to dedicate yourself
Enough to say you would
Live for someone...
That's a whole other mindset.

# Brightest Future

Just as wind amplifies fire,
Your heart does mine.
Let's go ahead and speak our vows.
Let's make the most of our time.

I don't ever want to lose you.
You are my other half.
I want you to know you complete me.
Please, don't ever leave me.

# Full Moon

Phase Two

# A Million Roses

In a room so dark, of course my thoughts begin to grow
wayward.
The question of whether I'd save your life or
That of a million strangers plagues my thoughts.
How can I live with the blood of a million people on my
hands?
But, how could I live without you?
You mean the world to me;
Yet, one life is worth far less than a million people.
Yet, you wrapped your rope of love around my heart;
If I was faced with this impossible choice,
With tears falling from my eyes,
I'd buy a million roses,
One for each funeral I would have to attend.

## Astonishment

I wish to the stars,
To freeze us in this very second.
Time often moves too fast when we're together.
The same stars that look down in disbelief at our joy.
We burn brighter and hotter than the summer months.
Peering into your heart of gold,
I realize I couldn't be more complete
Than right now.

## Simple Days

Take a walk with me
And I'll point out all
The beautiful things I see—
Simple things we often miss.

# Fatta

Sit here,
And let me share a lesson of love.
With love, you will have to make difficult decisions.
Some of which may seem impossible.
But know this...


For if you truly loved a flower,
You wouldn't pick it out of the ground to keep for yourself.
Keeping it would deprive it of its fellow flowers.
Eventually, it would wilt,
And your selfish hunt for love will have killed it.
If you truly loved that flower,
You would do what is best for it and leave it free.


For if you truly loved a songbird,
You wouldn't confine it to a cage too small.
Doing so would mean you separate it from its family.
The only song it would sing is of wanting to be released,
And how much it misses its family.
Caging it with no hope of escape would kill it.
If you truly loved that songbird,
You would do what is best for it and leave it free.

As much as you love something,
Sometimes, you are not what is best for it.
Love is not about having it your way,
It is about doing whatever is necessary for the benefit of another.
Even if what benefits the person,
Is at the sad expense of losing you.
Love is like construction,
Sometimes you have to tear yourself down
And build something magnificent from the debris.


When you understand this,
You will see more than anything that love is a sacrifice.
And those unwilling to lose something now
to gain more later,
Will lose everything in time.

## Service

Keep your service,
Let me take the reins of this wild horse
We call Life.
The same horse that may run rampant
At times, but with you I don't mind being out of control.
Let us not plan for the second that has yet to be born.
Here, and now, let me serve you.

## Moment

If I could paint a picture
Of that one encounter,
I would.
It seems like we live a life
That's far too short
Waiting for moments that pass
All too fast.
The only place that moment lives,
Is in my mind.
A feeling so intense that a camera
Couldn't even hope to capture it.
Words could never describe it.
It only took one moment,
And, of course, I am hooked forever.

# Blue Jay

Beautiful Blue Jay,
Why did you visit me on this beautiful day?
This day where the clouds look softer,
And the sun shines brighter,
And the air seems fresher.

Beautiful Blue Jay perched in my tree,
What brought you here?
Your coat of blue feathers makes my heart
Pound with excitement.
You didn't fly past,
But you stayed and allowed me to view your elegance.
The sun shines on you,
Like a spotlight on the lead in a musical.
Beautiful Blue Jay perched in my tree,
For what reason did you come?
The smile on my face,
Is a result of none other than YOU.
You came and brought happiness.
A regular morning became ever so eventful,
And I owe it all to you.

Beautiful Blue Jay,
You looked in my eyes as I did yours.
As you flew away,
I didn't feel sad.
I know our relationship will only grow stronger with time.
Clearly, you came to bring an old friend happiness.
I know you'll be back.
Until then, keep spreading your joy.
And when you return,
You'll still have a friend in me.

# Bliss of the Moment

Fill my day with blissful wonders,
Ones that come and stay.
Give me happiness with no strings.
No worries about tomorrow
Shall ever surface, because today
Is where I'll spend my time.
This is the calm before a storm that shall
Never show, no sadness will be here.
I sit and wonder who am I as the daybreak
Can now be seen.
Give me happiness with no strings.
A bliss filled day is what I see.
No problems will arise if I close my eyes
To the terrors of real life.
I cover my face to all that's bad because
Knowledge leads to pain,
And ignorance is a lovable friend.
What a day, what a day, indeed.
Where happiness shall come and never leave.

## Surprise

You strike my heart
In the weirdest of times.
How can I live without you?
I don't ever want to leave.
You turn the most regular days,
Into the most beautiful of experiences.

# Orange Moon

There are no words that can describe you tonight.
Instead of racking my brain
for words that haven't been invented,
Let me sit here and just admire you.
To speak of your breathtaking sight,
Would only downplay how I really feel.

I hate that the words just simply don't exist.
To have so much to say, yet not a single word holds the weight of
my heart.
So for now, for tonight,
Let me not speak,
Let me watch you, as you leave me speechless.

# My Utopia

Utopia can be defined as an imagined place or state of things in
which everything is perfect.
Perfection, such a grand prize.
As my eyes widened at the thought of perfection, I began to chase
it.
I wanted to find Utopia at all costs.


Before I left in search of Utopia,
I kissed your forehead and promised you a brighter future.
I believed to find my Utopia, I needed to travel.
I needed to venture off to
beautiful places with various luxuries.
Yet, no matter the location, something didn't feel right,
Almost as if something was missing.


While lying on a beach,
I thought of how your smile brightened my day
far more than the sun.
While observing the night sky full of stars,
I kept thinking that those stars don't compare to the beauty in
your eyes.
While listening to various instruments played live at concerts,
I couldn't help but remember the greatest sound on Earth Is your
laugh.

I can't believe I fell victim to this trap.
Searching for greener grass, I missed something that was directly
in front of me.
I chased Utopia hoping that my heart would feel everything
around me is perfect.
However, the only time I felt that everything was perfect was
when I was right next to you.


I guess what I'm trying to say is,
I'm sorry for my journey without you.
I traveled all around the world,
Only to realize that the grandest prize is you.
You, my dear, are My Utopia.

## Star Struck

Everything is different now.
Together we made a living.
A heart is what I gave to you.
A home is what you gifted me.
That night was so special.
I'm star struck looking in your direction.
Together we are now—
Let's not think about what tomorrow will bring.

## Sunrise Not Sunset

Your looks are more stunning than the sunrise.
When I'm around you, time does fly.
When you leave, I want to cry.
When I hold you, I could just die.
May our time together never end—unlike the sunset.

# The Deep End

Can you see the wheels turning in my head?
The friction of my mind turning
like two sticks starting a fire.
Questions that you nor I can even begin to solve.
If we are doomed to sit in this boiling pot of life,
And only one of us can escape,
Which of us should it be?

Do we become crab-like and say either all escape or none?
Or do we fight like two strangers
both wanting the same pair of shoes in a store?
If we both hang from the ledge of sins,
And I slip and plummet to the next life,
How long before you forget me?
Can I count on you to keep me in your thoughts?
Or will the noise of every day push me to drown in the deep end
of your mind?

I can't imagine being without you.
Simple things like eating would lose their purpose.
If the instance occurs where I am in danger,
And the only way to save me is
to put yourself in harm's way,
What would you do?

Are we not one and the same?

Would you hear my voice
if I called you from the other side?

# Cherry Tree

It's like we're walking blindfolded,
Unsure of what tomorrow will bring.
Do we fear our destination?
Should we dread our fate?
Can we avoid our sentencing?
Sitting under our Cherry Tree,
Speaking of sour days that may never
Come to fruition.
Each day leaping,
Hoping to be caught by the soft,
Caring hands of Mother Nature.
Wherever we go,
Whether near or far,
May this Cherry Tree remind us
That we are tied together
Like animals to their herd.
Who's to say where we'll end?
All I know is whom I'll be there with.

## Confession

You're everything I need.
Like a suit for the astronaut in space.
So pure and sweet like honey drops—
How do I not confess my love tonight?
Everything just feels so right.

# Mountains

In the mountains above, I
Waited for you.
Peering beyond the illustrations
Of a life I know nothing of.
Hoping to catch a gaze as glamorous
As the stars in your eyes.
From the clouds, I transcend.
Into your arms, I find home.
Every second without you,
Has led to this very moment—
This moment, when the stars above align,
And everything just feels so right.

# From Sand to Glass

How long have you been
The person of my dreams, you ask?
Curiosity paints itself on your face.
I motion to my wine glass.
For before this was glass,
This was sand on a beach.
Before that, it was sand under the ocean.
Before that, you were all I could think of.
In truth, I loved you long before this was
Transformed from grains of sand into glass.

# Persuasion of the Ocean

I hear the water yelling out to me
Begging me to return.
In its voice, it sounded desperate.
The crashing waves roared
My name louder each time.
Behind me, I see the water
Chasing the inner me.
Eager for me to return to its lair.

# Gone, But Not Lost

With love in my right hand,
And hope in my left,
And your name engraved on my heart,
I look to the stars and heavens above.
Eager to explore,
Yet sorrowful to leave you.
May this moment not be remembered
By the tears streaming down our faces.
Remember this moment not by the darkness
Of my departure,
But remember only by the light of a
Better tomorrow.
If you should ever feel alone
In this world of lost connections,
Recall that you live in my mind and my heart.
Tonight, we sing a song of remembrance.
Tonight, we party as if it were our last time on Earth.
Tonight, we reach for the stars from home;
Tomorrow, I reach for you from the stars.

Every night, look to the stars that I shall send your way.
Each star in the sky above stands for a reason I love each of you.
My lovely family, I leave you with this;
Missing you is an understatement.
I will grieve over not having you within arm's length.
I will fall apart each and every morning,
Knowing I cannot share my dreams with you.
I will plummet into the darkest abyss
without you to save me.
And after I fall, break, and tear,
I will remember this very moment,
I will remember the love I see in your eyes right now.
Then...
I will smile brighter than the sun, knowing
The names tattooed across my heart
Are millions of miles away,
Yet, it will feel like you are right by my side.
Thank you—
I love you.

## Patience

No longer do I hide my heart from my mind.
Could this day be any more perfect?
To the rich, go the spoils,
And to the patient, go the lovely.
You are the reward I could never imagine...
The book I never want to put down...
The person I cannot live without...
Patience pulled us together.
Here's to an eternity of oneness.

## Unspoken Love

We don't open our mouths,
Yet the depth of our conversation is surreal.
Our minds speak on a level of connection
Beyond all words.
Neither of us have spoken.
Yet, I know exactly how you feel.
Our silence is our strength.
We understand that words are misleading,
So we choose not to break the silence—
And yet, I have never understood you more.

## Below the Surface

I may never understand it.
How could I when understanding myself
Has eluded me all these years?
I don't want to understand it.

Beyond my thoughts are my feelings.
And those drive me more than logic ever could.
This connection is deeper than my understanding.
What lies miles below the surface of our love,
Will only be discovered in time.

## Two Doves

Two Doves, meant to be together,
Both powerful on their own,
Together are invincible,
Yet, apart they will be forever.

Two Doves, flying in opposite directions,
Looking back all the way,
Troubled times ahead,
Yet, ahead they strive to.

Two Doves, facing the hardest of times,
Yell out to each other with no stop;
Searching for love, they come together,
And realize that love shall last forever.

# Glass Made

What will be left of us
If the passion dies out?
Will our wildfire of love
Become a dimly lit flame?
Or worse, will our electricity
Shatter like glass?
Leaving me to pick up the shards of
Our hearts.
Pieces that will never amount to a whole again.
What if our love fails?

# Hoping for a Future

Here I am,
Back riding the same horse.
Hoping for a different outcome.
Unsure of what future I even want.

Here we are,
Singing the same songs.
When will our star burn out?
Leaving us to freeze alone.

Whatever the future may hold,
Even if it ends with "us" as a memory,
Should this be our last ride?
I'm glad we tried again.

This way, I won't have the question
Lingering in my head.
This way, if we do fail,
At least I know we gave it our all.

# Fill My Heart

It's 1:12 a.m.,
And this feeling seeps deeper inside me,
like rainwater through cracks on the ground.
This feeling is something I've only read about.
It's scary, but isn't fear a good thing?

When I need to smile, I just look at you.
Everything about you brings happiness into my life.
I don't think you know what you do to me,
but please never leave me.

I need you to hold me closely,
To kiss me slowly,
To love me forever.

You don't just complete me, you shape me.
You make me want to be so much better than
I thought I could be.
The warm feeling I get in my chest when I am with you...

That feeling is indescribable.
That feeling is more special than anything in the world.
That feeling is ten times as powerful as love.

I admit, I was searching for love,
Yet, I found something far greater—
I found you.
And you fill my heart like an infinity pool.

What more do I need in this world?
So long as I have you, I'm happy.

For what is my heart without your hand to hold it?
Well, what is a pen with no ink?
Useless...purposeless.
I asked you to fill my heart,
And of course, you found a way to overflow it.

It's 6:15 a.m.,
And you never left my mind,
And my heart has never been more full.

# Waning

Phase Three

# Sleep Pt.2 - Nightmare

The most amazing sight in the world is your eyes.
I look deep into them as I hold your right hand
in my left.
Looking around, I see we are surrounded by bright orange and
purple tulips.
It seems so surreal, but isn't everything supposed to feel this way
when I'm around you?
To my right, I see more flowers,
breathtaking to say the least.

Looking back to my left, I miss the gaze of your eyes.
Suddenly, you're gone and my left hand that was clasped around
your right hand is now empty.
As I turn in circles, I see no trace of you.
On my knees now, I begin to cry out your name.
The flowers that once surrounded me have disappeared, leaving
only an abyss of darkness.
Calling out to you in this pit of emptiness,
tears roll down my face as I realize... I am all alone.

## Divided

These moments are the hardest I've ever faced.
A house divided against itself is a problem
that can be fixed,
But what about a mind divided?
What's the solution for that?

Stuck between a rock and a hard place,
who will rescue me?
I'm between wanting to show all my emotions,
and not wanting to lose our friendship.
Should I ask if we ever had a chance?
Will you even respond?

Or should I hold my thoughts in because, in truth,
neither answer would satisfy me?
But I need to know, what do you think of me?
Am I just a cloud in your mind that gets whisked away when you
think of another?
Is our friendship even worth saving?

Sitting on a wall afraid of the direction I'll fall,
afraid to even lean.
On one side, a pack of savage wolves;
on the other, a herd of hungry lions.
Either choice will cause pain.
But sitting here divided will be the death of me.

## Raindrop

I am but a simple drop of water,
Falling from God knows where.
Unsure of my purpose,
But I hope I'm doing right.
Battling with life at every corner,
Did you intend to be my adversary?
Still searching for my purpose.
Is it just to fall on your command?
When I clash with the earth
I hope to fulfill my purpose.
Yet I can't help but ponder
The choices we made to get here.
Plummeting from our peak,
Like a drop from the sky above.
Like I'm falling from heaven itself.
Like the sun colliding with Earth.
Neither of us can figure out this situation.
Life, too complicated of an equation
For either of us to even begin to solve.
So, like the simple raindrop,
Sadly, I will continue to fall.

# I Dreamed of You Last Night

I had a dream that I was all by myself.
I had a dream that nobody else cared.
I had a dream that I was all alone.
Then, I woke up and realized that it was real!

# Deception

I dove into your eyes to get to your mind.
There, I saw us and our future together.
Almost as if I was watching a TV show.
I saw this in you every second we shared together.

Yet, I never saw this possibility playing out.
For some reason, your eyes deceived me.
Making me believe your heart
And mine would forever be intertwined.

## Answered Calls

I'll never understand you.
You called for peace, love, and happiness,
And I answered those calls.
Yet, here we are...
In two different beds.
Residing in two different spaces.
Living two different lives.

## Change

I fear that we will change.
Twenty years will pass, and
We are no longer the same.
We will grow apart.
So far, in fact, our bond will be beyond saving.

# Intangible

I can touch my shirt,
And I can feel it.

I can touch my hair,
And I can feel it.

I can touch my leg,
And I can feel it.

Strangely enough, I cannot touch love,
Yet, I can feel it.
Or at least, I can feel the lack of it coming from you.

# Broken Love

I hate when you talk
Because I know you're going to say something
I don't agree with.
I hate opening my mouth to speak,
Because I know you don't even want to hear me.

So, I write these words knowing it's the only time I'm in control.
We will continue to argue.
You're going to escalate your voice,
And I'll do the same to mine.

At the end of the hour, the wine bottle will be empty,
And your heart and mine will be broken.
You head left, and I head right—
All because you and I couldn't get past this fight.

# Apathy For You

My heartbeat slows as I
Drift to sleep at the thought of you.
The worries once attached to you
No longer concern me in any way.
I can feel myself becoming more and more detached
From the emotions that filled my once caring heart.
Seeing you is no longer like a drug I am addicted to.
Through no fault of yours or mine,
I don't see the joy that I once lived for
In your eyes anymore.
To call our bond broken would be like calling
The ocean, a simple body of water.
Unaware of the vast amount of life forms
That make the ocean what it truly is.
So where do I go from here?
Drifting in the field of bleakness, I couldn't
Hope to see the light anymore.
But I shan't worry.
I no longer feel connected to the light.
My bond with the light is no different than
My severed bond with you.
What good is the light
If I don't feel its warmth?

# Lost Journal Entry of a Black Man #1

**(Enslaved, Year 1855)**

To be held in chains, stripped of what it means to be human is a
burden no man should bear.
To perform manual labor for nothing in return but ridicule is
insanity.
To be forced against your will to do tasks with no future other
than to do it all over again the next day is inhumane.
But, then again, we aren't really human to you, are we?

I wonder what would be the reaction of these slave owners if they
put themselves in our shoes; nay, in our chains and answer this:
"Is this how you want your life to be?  Do you want your children
to be enslaved this way? ... Like the Israelites were in Egypt"?
Sadly, if they did try to envision their life being as broken as ours,
they wouldn't care.
It wouldn't be real enough to them.
It won't be real enough until they are picking cotton on the fields
as their hands bleed and as their feet burned.

Only then would they look at us as more than property.
But I do assure you, that if the choice was up to us Negros, they
would pray we don't enslave them.

# *Voice*

My voice retreats to the back of my throat.
I wouldn't dare say the words I truly feel.
What you think is me tucking my tail between my legs,
Is me avoiding the seventh argument of the day.
I chose not to speak hoping silence would save our bond.
I had so many thoughts spinning around,
That my head felt like a tornado.
Who knew silence could be just as deadly as the knife that tore
our relationship.
Then again, everything with you seems to be lethal to our
connection.
My silence may have been an issue,
But your voice was the Achilles heel in our love.

# H.M.W.H

I'll never understand
How someone so amazing
Can be so sinister inside.

If you can fly, fly.
Don't give false hope,
Like an eagle teaching a worm to soar.
No, more like a vulture
Befriending a dying animal.
You're everything I need,
And you know it.
Being with you is like
*Honey Mixed With Hell.*
Do I enjoy our sweet,
Finite moments together?
How can I when after,
It'll be hell trying to forget you?
Falling for you was my own fault.
How can you knowingly harm me?
I guess I'll never understand
How someone so breathtaking
Can be so evil inside.

# Snowball Effect

My words are ruby stones.
Please don't make them blood diamonds.
It seems like I'm changing,
But I promise, you caused this.
Any alteration in my persona,
Is the insignificant snowball
You created that slowly, but surely,
Gained speed and size down the mountain.
Oh life, what a slippery slope!
You ignited this snowball effect.
You, and you alone, are to blame for this tragedy.

# The Way You See Me

I could cry you a river,
And you would say I am trying to drown you.
If I gave you flowers,
You would say I tried to steal your heart.
I can give you all the light in the world,
Yet, all you would focus on is the shadow my light will cast.
If I did reach for the moon,
You would say I'm trying to get away from you.

Who I am, and who you see me as are two different people.
I let your view of me distract me and who I really am.
And yes, I'm over caring.
And yes, sometimes it may seem like I don't care enough.
But the way you view me isn't just wrong, it is ridiculous, to say
the least.
Why should I keep convincing you of my love?
When you can't even see me for me.

# Worst Days

I wish you could see me on my worst days,
When I'm home and the cameras aren't rolling,
When I'm alone and the lights are turned off.

My smile and my laughter are only a mask,
One that I wear oh so well.
Of course, you would never know;
I doubt you even care.

During the day, I may act carefree,
Oh what a facade you believe.
If you looked beyond my surface,
Deep into my eyes,
I promise you'd see a small child curled up wiping away tears,
I cry.

Please don't judge me simply because I'm giving you my truth.
I'm telling you, I'm like a full moon,
The only side you see of me is the light,
Unbeknownst to you, the other half is just as dark.

Isn't every coin double-sided?
Doesn't every story have two views?
I refuse to dot another "i" or cross another "t,"
Until you accept me... the somber me.

# Hiding from What?

We run from the flames of reality.
Each step like crossing a minefield.
To face the music
Is to admit our failures.
I'd rather not sing that
Melancholy song today.
So, we keep running
From the reality we hate to face.
Conjuring new thoughts to
Replace unsavory ones.
The light shines on us—no more truths
To hide, even from ourselves.
Truths that make this reality
A horrible nightmare.
So, we run from the flames of reality.
Knowing the light will soon shine,
On the sins we cloak with darkness.

## Equity

We are all going to fall.
When that happens, I hope we all land on flat ground.
That way no one is higher than another.
Each of us, regardless of race, gender, or religion will be on the
same level as the person next to us.
If this were to happen,
Would you change your perspective?
Or would you still chase money and power?
Since we are all equal,
you couldn't use any of that to rise above us.
If all your money, your possessions, and your job disappeared this
instant,
what would you have left of yourself?
I guess we won't know until you fall on equal ground as those you
oppress.

# The Box

I can feel the box
They put us in.
Like a mime, the box
Is invisible but restraining.
If you are not like me
You won't feel the barrier.
This invisible prison won't apply to you.
Even though your people placed it on us.
Invisible like the air
Yet solid like concrete.
Limiting us in all our actions.
This box is a death sentence.
And you refuse to admit it.

## Forbidden Love

Neither of us can answer this question.
Our love is like a twisted riddle—
A joke neither of us gets—
Or a maze we just can't escape.
Who told us what we can't be?
Why is our love something
No one wants to see?

## Halted in Life

Stuck in the quicksand of
My thoughts as I cannot
Find the answer to my question.
You, nor I, can solve the riddle
That is poison to my mind.
So, what now?
Life gets up and passes me,
As I continue to sink.

# Empty Arms

Like a lioness, I patiently await
For my time to strike.
Unsure of what the result will be,
So, I contain myself.
Failure sings its sorrowful
Tune in my head.
Crouched in the tall grass
As I calculate success' chance.
For years I've studied,
And it's high time I make my move.
Planned out years in advance,
I see everything falling into place.
Triumph isn't probable,
But anything is better than
The zero chance of not trying.
Of course, I watch my plan crumble before me.
I hang my head in defeat.
Failure's voice echoes off
The walls in my head.
Still not mad at the outcome.
Just tired of trying to give my all to something,
And being left with nothing.

## I Know You

No, you're not the killer.
You're the rope my great ancestors hung from.
The wood they burned from.
The chains we are still in.
The bullet that always seems to kill us.
The nightmare that only haunts us.
You can't admit it.
No, you won't admit it.
Yes, you are far from the killer.
But the blood on your hands is mighty visible.

## Ending of Us

You'll be the death of me.
And I'll be the birth of you.
We'll keep on arguing,
'Cause nothing between us is new.

## Forget

You're not just anybody—
You're the part of me
I've tried to forget.

# The Knife in My Back

I could tear down
Your walls of security.
In an instant, everything
You built would come crashing down.
Leaving you in distress
And turmoil, with no end in sight.
Can you imagine being in
That scenario?
With your mental and physical health
In the palm of my hand.
Forced to do my bidding
Like a puppet to the puppeteer.
You would hate living in that reality,
One where I choose to break you down.
So why are you doing it to me?
Why are you demolishing my
Walls of peace and
Crushing my floors of hope?
If the roles were flipped, you
Wouldn't want me doing it to you.
So why, why are you focused on breaking me?

## Tears for Kobe

Let the sky forever be dark with no sun to shine.
Let blood fall from black clouds and may it burn your skin to the
touch.
Let fire rise from under you.
Let lightning strike you down.

Remove your heart from your chest before life does it for you.
Emotions will serve to be a weakness; one you cannot afford.
Let tears for the great one drop like heavy stones.
Let my tears never stop.

# Frozen

How do you cry in the snow?
Tears turn to 'sicles as they flow.
Oh, how hard tragedy has struck you.
Forced to live with burdens placed by others.

Oh, how hard it is to breathe.
The effect feels like two elephants sitting on your lungs.
What happens when there's a fork in the road?
What if neither path is desirable?
Going back to being just a tall tale that is not an option.

In the wake of this disaster,
Your tears fall in the snow.
Decaying inside leads to your eyes seeing
Darkness and even your heart begins to grow cold.

# Gullible

I'm susceptible to the reality you feed me.
Whether a truth spills,
Or a lie flies from you,
I cannot tell.
Your word is your currency.
For each truth you tell,
You gain.
Each lie you mutter,
You lose.
If this was our reality,
All your riches would disappear.

# Soulless

One day,
You will wake up
and none of the people
around you will be there anymore.
Those bridges have all
Been burned long ago.
Every mistake will haunt your nights.
Sleepless nights will become
As plentiful as nights are restless.
Laughter becomes a foreign
Action you know nothing of.
Empty and alone as the walls
Seem bare and the floors are cold.
Reaching out for help is
A lost art you cannot even attempt.

## Facade

What's behind that
Amazing smile of yours?
The secrets you hide
Are more valuable than gold.
If only I could peer into your mind.
On the outside you're so perfect,
But I know you're crumbling behind that mask.

## Defeated

Why does it rain over me?
Looking up, I can see the dark gray clouds hovering over me.
My eyes sting as tears roll from them.
Another dark day; another dark day.

Rain on my parade, I have no reason to be here anyway.
The rain only brings more problems.
Please, rain, won't you stop controlling me?
Each drop from above grants a new mountain to climb.

## Challenges

Life's test is too challenging.
Your test is beyond my ability.
The weight of it all crushes
Me each time I give it my all.
Tucking my tail between my legs
As I return to the hole from which I came.

## Starving for More

We ingest the lies
We're fed each day.
Starving for the truth,
But we intake whatever is given.
If we question the plate in front of us,
Are we defiant in our paths?
Either we don't eat and starve.
Or, we are satisfied with being misled.
Each plate, another round of stories—
Waiting on the truth to be given.

# Weird Air

You, nor I, did anything wrong.
But, when we are in these awkward moments,
With nothing to say because anything out of our lips would be
awkward.
We stare at the walls because looking at each other would be all-
the-more taboo.
In these moments, when no one is around and we are mere feet
apart,
I don't want to breathe around you.
I don't want to intake the air that once was yours.
I feel that you are a glass of cold milk,
And I am a lactose-intolerant child seconds from dying of thirst.
In that instant, the child would have to decide...
die of thirst or drink something and deal with the unfortunate
outcome.
I don't want to breathe the weird air around you.
I refuse to take any more in.
You, nor I, did anything wrong,
But I refuse to drink from the glass of milk.

# Warmth of the Night

I remember those nights,
Back when you were so cold
And I was your only warmth.

Oh, what I would give to be back.
Too often I reminisce over you.
I can't help hoping to have you again.

Foolish or not, I'm still here.
Listening to our favorite song,
While I sit on the beach watching the waves crash.
The same way we used to do together.
Back when I held you so tight,
That my body warmth was your sun.
I remember those nights—
You?

# Red Pen

I am writing this in Red.
Do you feel that?
Neither do I.
It was never real.
Real is the Red blood in my veins.
Real is the Red apple that can be likened
To you being the apple of my eye.
Real is the Red ink used to write these words
Of disgrace.
This is me...Red.
I am at rock bottom, Red.
Why Red?
Why Red?
Why Red?
How heartless are you?
Wretched like a witch.
Tell me what spell you cast.
To leave me powerless and in pain.
You truly are a monster.
I do not write in Red...
Unless a bond is unsalvageable.
Goodbye Red.

# 1/26/20

Ya know, the irony in love
Is that at any moment the unexpected can happen,
And that very same love will instantly transform
Into a pain beyond any measure.

# A Dollar With A String On The End

Wrap your mind around this reality,
Trying to survive in a world not meant for me.
Everything that attracts me
Seems to be more a deception and less a reality.

## Pieces of Myself

The taste of wine
Like a waterfall down my throat.
Numb and distorted,
My vision becomes.
How do I pull myself
Back together...
When each part of
Me is separating?

## Our Time

I want to
Write you a poem.
I want to
Sing you a song.
I fear it's too late.
Has our time really come and gone?

# Cloth of a Peasant

I haven't much to give to this world.
Broken by life and kicked to the curb
Like a stray cat as I find home under the bridge.
Spat on and kicked by each passerby.

Leaving me to question,
What more can life take from me?
I have no physical possessions,
Not even a shirt or pair of pants to call my own.

This instant I could take my final breath,
And no one would ever remember me.
They would look at my lifeless body and step over me,
As if I'm a hurdle in their path.
The dirt on my back is the closest thing I have to a possession,
And I'm forever grateful for it.
For this peasant has seen the slums of this wretched world,
And knows more than the man whose head lies rest to the crown.

Should I die this instant?
Let it be known that when the world has taken everything from
me,
I never lost the cloth of my mind.
The mind of this peasant is worth more than that of a king,
Blind to the reality of the suffering man.

# My First Crime

When did I commit my first crime?
My shaking hand on the Bible as I watch the tears fall down my
mother's face.
To my left resides a jury, and not one of them looks like me.
The word guilty is shouted from the foreperson.

Sentenced to life in prison for a crime I did not commit.
The chains wrapping around my wrist are cold
As I'm being pushed farther away from my parents.
Now I wonder if the true crime I did commit,
Was being born Black in a white country.

# Crow

Our only goal...
Escaping to freedom.
Rapidly rushing,
Fearing for our lives.
Each step we take
Is tied with fate.
Fate, what a sad
One I see for us.
The squawk of the *Crow*
Sounds when we
Thought we were free.
Free, how can I
Even imagine that?
Sprinting for the border.
In the blanket of the night.
But the *Crow* sees us.
It sees the success
We can achieve.
*Crow*, was your sole
Purpose in creation to destroy us?

Attached to us like
A nail hammered to a board.
*Crow*, why does your Creator
Bring us so much harm?
Can you not see
Our lives are being lost?
No, our lives are being taken!
Snatched out of our bodies
With ropes to hang us and
Your guns for us to kill ourselves.
*Crow*, why doth thou not alloweth us to be free?
*Crow*, doth thou despise us so?
*Crow*, why art thou making us bleed?
Please, we just want to live, *Crow*.

# Fate

I'm just saying fate is a twisted lady.
What if I'm not good enough?
Do I then fall prey to the wolves?  Like a fly trapped in honey,
Or perhaps a fish in the claw of a bear,
I feel condemned to a fate chosen by someone else.
I feel that I can do everything right in this world,
And yet, someone else can take my life.
Unarmed, yet in their eyes
A target lies on my race.
I'm just saying, is this really our fate?

# Mortals and Mistakes

Both partners are sick of their relationship.
Repetitive arguments begin to
Take a toll on the young couple.

Sleeping back-to-back
Is becoming far too common.
Previously, they both said things, in fights,
That never should have been said.

Now, silence fills the halls
Morphing the warm palace
Into a cold silent dungeon.
Lovelessness seeps deeper into the walls.

Yet, to friends they confess their
Love for each other runs deep.
To each other, they say all the wrong things.
Now, they say nothing at all.
Both, too proud to speak first;
Both, unwilling to keep fighting.
Now they're fully separated.
If only they would understand each other now.

I find it ridiculous that mortals have no true power.
And yet their pride measures the distance
Of a shadow cast by the sun before it sets.
And the sun will set on them... sooner than they think.

# Don't Talk Anymore

Have you realized
That we don't talk anymore?
That when we walk by each other,
Not even a glance between the two of us exists?

The fire that burned was never strong,
But I always did just enough to keep it lit.
Somewhere along the way, I adopted your attitude.
I stopped trying to ignite a fire with these two dampened sticks.

No, we don't talk anymore.
But our solitude is different.
You have a million thoughts in your head,
And not one is about me.
Your solitude is pleasure.

No, we don't talk anymore,
But our solitude is different.
I have a million thoughts in my head,
And every one is about you.
My solitude is sorrowful.

Truthfully, I feel like I'm drowning.
And you are there, watching me drown.
But you don't save me,
And I don't ask you to either.
Because we don't talk anymore.
And I have to respect that.

Today, I really needed your help,
Habitually, I grabbed my phone.
I stopped and stared at your contact information.
I can see the last time we texted was months ago.

I typed the message about how badly I needed you,
But I couldn't press send.
No, we don't talk anymore.
And I know you would prefer it that way.

# Garden

That garden is perfect.
The lilies are breathtaking.
The roses are beyond beautiful.
The sunflowers are magnificent.
The lotuses are deeply enchanting.
The orchids are golden and mesmerizing.

I walk to the field of flowers.
As I stand in the center of them all,
I see that this garden
Is no longer perfect.
Its middle lies waste to a foreign object.
Gorgeous is this field when
I am not a part of it.

I turn to leave for fear of ruining it more.
I hope my imprint is not too large.
Staring from afar, I do notice
That the garden is perfect.

## Thorns of You

I reached out for the Rose
Yet, it was the thorns I met.
Its beauty—a fantasy.
Its pain—a reality.
I wonder what hurt the Rose.
I wonder what cut the Rose so deeply
It spouted thorns to never let one close again.
Can I break through the thorns to see its beauty?
Perhaps I'm the very reason the thorns are in place.

## Dark Rooms

What they don't tell you
Is that in the dark, all the answers are there—
Hidden like eggs on Easter.
Waiting to be uncovered like clues to a detective.
When sight is not available,
Our minds reach for answers we are too blind to see.

## Reminiscing

I miss those days—
When you were sad,
You ran to me.
When you were glad,
You skipped my way.
When you were lost,
I was your compass.
Where did the time go?
When did we change?

# Switch

Really listen to what I have to say.
Sometimes I wonder if I were you, and you were I,
Would I treat you the way you treat me?
You treat me like I am a mere afterthought.
Do I really bother you that much?

If the roles were reversed and I had this powerful grip on you,
Would I look at you as a bug to be stepped on?
That is how you view me.
Or would I treat you as if a wall separates us and simply never
acknowledge you?

If I were you and you were I,
What would I do, you ask?
Even though I know how poorly you treated my heart,
If the rolls were flipped, I'd look you in your eyes and tell you how
much you mean to me.

# Tragedy of the Butterfly

Butterflies emerge as the most beautiful creatures on Earth.
And I am a butterfly with all the beauty in the world;
Yet, I retreat back into my cocoon for fear of falling.
Afraid to try to fly and fail—I don't try at all and, wilt and die.

# A Wilted Flower

(As a tear drops from my face)
A quiet sob is the worst sob.
When you scream out your lungs,
Yet no one can hear a thing.

As the fatal blow of reality hits,
You lie crushed and defeated.
As Death whispers in your ear.

Begging for a helping hand,
Instead, you receive a knife in your back.
Face down in a pillow as you cry.

(The tear hits the ground)
My body hits the ground, too, as I die.
I feel for your tears as if they are my own.
For I know that I'm dead, but sadly you, you're all alone.

## Breaking

Bones that break
Are strong forever.
Bonds that break
Are gone forever.

## Poison

The sour taste of life drips
Down the back of my throat.
Time cannot heal the poison
I'm forced to ingest each day.

## Chaos

When the rocks come crashing down,
Oh how sad events can become;
In the heart of this chaos,
No eye of the storm exists.

## Shared Pain

Don't make this harder
Than it already is.
Let's both just hurt today.
But please, don't make me
Relive this tomorrow.

# Moonlight

Please continue to cover me—
I wear your shine like a cloak,
And you protect me like a shield.
Perched up in the night sky,
You look so magnificent.

You feel so close,
Almost as if I can reach out and touch you.
But we both know that can't happen.
Unable to touch, I'll admire you from afar, but please,
Don't stop casting your light.

# What Now?

I try to do me,
And that is never good enough.
I attempt to be you,
And still, I fall far short.

In my head,
I can succeed.
But in reality,
I fear it will never work.

Frustration boils out of me.
Anger follows close behind.
Yet, my inner feeling is defeat.
For a failure I seem to be.

# Are We Living?

The cost of life—
Are we even truly living?
Apart from you, I find a hole
In the place my heart should be.
Our distance is lethal.
Closing my eyes, I see you clearly.
I can still smell your sweet fragrance.
If I were a thief in the night,
Your heart would be my only goal.
If you were locked in a tower,
Believe that I am here to free you.
Yet, here we are.
I turn in my head trying to fill this hole.
I cannot believe this is life.
How can I even call this living?

# Fault in our Words

I hate the art of spoken word.
From my lips to your ears
Only trouble occurs.
What is said can never be unspoken
Nor unheard.
It is far too permanent.
Like ink you chose to stitch on your skin
While intoxicated,
Spoken word is a mistake.
It is hateful and rash.
Yes, I hate the art of spoken word
Because what's said will linger forever.

## Silence

Why is it
When the silence sets in
And the darkness of the night creeps in,
You are all I can think of?

## Anaphora of the Lonely

I wish the world
To leave me alone.
To carry oneself
To carry one's own.
In this world of sins
We all atone.
I wish the world
To leave me alone.

# Sparring my Mind

Spinning in circles
Fighting a mind that refuses to give in.
Taking punches,
And falling face first.
Bruised,
But stopping is no longer an option.
Pushing forward through
The snow blizzard of life.
Begging for mercy.
Taking a final breath.
Unable to take another step.

# Decaying in Time

Millions of words to say each hour,
But who will listen to this lowly serf?
So much to give, yet no one to receive.
The pressure will continue to build.
And when it explodes,
Millions of ideas perish with me.

# Snake Skin

I wonder what it would take
To shed the skin of a sinner.
Unraveling like yarn no longer
Tethered to its spool.
Cloaked in the dirt of a life
None of us chose to live.
Where is the salvation for a slave?
Cryptic chains decorate our wrists
And necks like lights on a winter tree.

# Week With a Killer

I spent a week with a killer.
One that said I was like him.
But he expects better of me.

If I am like him,
Then aren't I a killer?
Even if not yet,
In time I may change.
I may become the man I fear.

So how can I be better?
If you don't want me to be like you,
Then why force this wrath upon me?
The very same wrath that he endured.
It's like he tells me to look straight ahead,
Then is enraged that I cannot see behind me.

I spent a week with a killer.
He made me this way.
Or could it be that I always wanted this.
Perhaps he shaped me.
Maybe I gave in to the urge.

Yes, I became a killer.
I barely resisted the temptation.
I wasn't born like this.
Yet, he shaped me this way.

I killed the killer.
Now, I am all that's left of him.
I spent a week with a killer.
And now I am no better than him.

# A Horror-Filled Folktale

Telling a story I should have never known.
A story that should have never been told to me.
The dark cloud over me pours cold rain.
Hopefully, it will wash over the land of many losses.
Things that were less lost and more so taken.
The rain can wash away what was there,
But we both know what happened is now a part of the land.

# Why Did I Cry?

I cried because it hurt.
It hurt to want nobody more than this one amazing person
And for that person to want nothing to do with me.
It hurt to be stuck between wanting you
And just wanting you to be happy.
Even though I know your happiness will never come from me.
I began to feel so helpless around you.
I crumbled like a building with a weak foundation.
I collapsed, and I needed an outlet.
I'm sorry—I caused our separation.
And when I realized this,
I cried because I knew things would never be the same.

## Acceptance

I hate that I love you.
I hate that I want to hold you.
I hate that I listen to music that reminds me of you.
I hate that I can only think about you.
I hate that I eat and the food has no taste anymore.
I hate that I want to have fun, but that means talking to you.
I hate that I know we don't talk.
I hate that I feared losing you.
I hate that I know that fear came true.
I hate that I don't sleep anymore.
I hate that I cry over you.
I hate that I always find things that remind me of you.
I hate that I always feel like something is missing.
But most importantly,
I hate that I have to accept the fact that you and I are over.

# With Watery Eyes

I think what hurts the most
Is that I will never be able to tell you "thank you."
I need you back; where did you go?

Until we meet again,
Should we ever meet again,
These tears will just have to do.

# Missing You

In the short time I knew you, you became so important to me.
Just yesterday we laughed 'til our stomachs cried.
The fun we had seemed so pure and genuine
Knowing you were beside me was like a shield to a soldier in
battle.


I was so blind to the feeling of knowing you;
I missed the ledge of reality in front of me.
Reality is, you're gone which leaves me to see that people are like
time,
Tied up in the moment, I didn't even realize you passed me by
until you were gone.
Man, what I wouldn't give for you to be here next to me
As we figure out this labyrinth we call life.


Being lost isn't so bad with you being inches away from me.
Talking to you was the rope that kept me tethered to sanity.
Without you, my mind will control me, instead of the other way
around.
I'm still a soldier in battle; only now I'm missing my shield.

Here I am, left to deal with the aftermath of our relationship.
I know I'm being selfish; I truly am happy for you.
You mean everything to me and it took you being gone
To learn what it means to truly be lost.
I reached out for you today; but, of course, I knew you weren't there.


I was hoping my eyes deceived me,
Hoping that if I closed my eyes the sweet smell of you would calm my nerves.
Sadly, the air that filled my lungs was cold and sharp
Like a twenty below zero winter in Russia.
Where am I going with this?


It feels like I'm stuck in quicksand scared and afraid,
But, I know, when I open my eyes, I'm not stuck in quicksand.
It just feels like something isn't right,
I don't know—maybe I'm just missing you.

# Hate Being Alone

I hate being alone.
When I am, my mind projects ten different versions of me.
Each of them argue amongst themselves over
Which is the best me.
Arguments that have been going on
For years, with still no end in sight.
Ten voices competing for the podium.
Leaving my head split in each direction.
The only thing they agree on,
Is that I am the worst form of us...
Of me.
So, they keep fighting.
I sit and listen to them describe my faults.
They list the reasons you left.
And, of course, I am the problem.
Being alone means hearing
My negative features from the person
Closest to me.
So yes,
I hate being alone.

# Jealous (Why Not I?)

If you draw a line in the sand,
How close am I to reaching it?
Am I so far off that your line is out of sight?
Am I even on the beach at all?

I know you took another's hand.
How did that person cross your line, the same line I fell so far
from?
Out of my eyes, I only see red.
If I'm a bull, your partner is the matador who doesn't leave the
arena alive.

I know I've never met them.
But in my mind that person is the serpent in your garden.
It may appear friendly.
But even Judas seemed friendly to Jesus.

Maybe, they are not a bad person.
Maybe, I feel this way because they accomplished something I
could not.
After all, they crossed your line of love and it isburied in your
heart.
And I am left to sit like a bird with a clipped wing.
Watching you both fly, wondering why you chose another, and
not I.

# Hearts Break and Flowers Wilt

What do words and I have in common?
The similarity may not seem clear,
But it is there, and it took me time to see it.
These words are not that different from me.

If I'm a flower, how can I grow without the sun?
Don't you see that you're my sunlight?
Yet, being without you is like an eclipse.
Constantly living in the shadow of an object.
But how can I even really call this living?
I'm a shell, a mere after image of who I once was.
I'm a wilted flower, soon to be abandoned from the garden.

Sometimes it hurts more than others.
Ninety percent of the time I can bear the pain.
But that ten percent...
That ten percent is harsher than the harshest of storms.
It produces the tallest, strongest waves that even the most skilled
sailors fear.
Knowing you and I are farther apart than the North is from the
South,
Burns me from the inside of my bones.

I, so badly, want to lock eyes with you,
And say those three words I never got the chance to utter.
Those three beautiful words that describe how I feel about you.
Words, that come to mind every time I think of you.

I feel the blood in my heart seeping out of the cracks.
My heartbeat is slow, but I'm far from calm.
You're a tornado that wrecked everything.
And the crazy thing is,
You left just enough of me alive so I can still feel.
I can still feel your hands in mine.
I can still feel the warmth from your body.
I can still feel the happiness I felt being with you.
It is faint, but not non-existent.

Words don't express this anymore.
Words just are not enough.
Words and I have that in common,
Because neither of us are enough for you.

## Dancing Alone

I'll keep dancing
Even if I don't have you with me physically.
Who's to say when I close my eyes, you're not here with me
mentally?
In my mind, you never left.
I'm refusing to stop the music.

Jamming to songs that remind me of you.
How will you ever leave my mind,
When I purposefully play songs to think of you?
I'll cross that bridge when I get there.
For now, I'll just keep dancing.

# An Endless Loop

Curling into a ball has become my home.
I can't even reminisce on what we had.
The memories of us are beginning to fade.
All I can remember is how you made me feel.
Where we went, and what we said are pointless.
As time moves on, I fall farther from reality.
I fall into a head space that feels so familiar.
It feels like I'm lost in nothingness.
I'm learning to find homage in the silence.
But the thoughts of you are so loud.
It feels like someone is screaming your name.
I try to block the yelling, but I can't.
I feel the wave rushing over me.
I need to find a way to escape the noise.
So, I begin to curl into a ball that has become my home.
I realize I can't even reminisce on what we had.
Because the memories of us are beginning to fade.
And the process starts all over again.

## Fences

I feel that they are different than me.
If they peek behind the curtain,
They will judge me at face value.
And I'm not ready for that.
I'm not ready for the public eye.

I don't know them,
So, I can't give them the chance to attack the inner me.
I rush to put walls up between us.
These walls that cover every side of me.
These walls that are too tall to peek over.
And, much too solid to knock down.
I cannot let you into my life.
I refuse to let you draw conclusions as to who I really am.

In the mirror, I see my once thick black hair,
Is now thinning and almost completely white.
I remember my youth and putting these walls up way back then.
Staring at these barriers I realize my last memory worth anything,
Was putting up these great dividers I see before my eyes.

I condemned myself to this section of the land.
Never reaching out.
Never trying anything new.
Never expanding my thoughts.
Never leaving the comfort of these walls.
I'm too old to even attempt to tear down the monster I put up.
What purpose did these fences serve?
So concerned about others and their views,
That I built walls to separate myself out of fear.
In actuality, all I did was build a prison.
I coddled myself for years.
I'm like a baby bird that never took the chance to fly.
Or like a gazelle that never learned to run from a lion.
So protected by these walls,
I never gave myself the chance to grow.
I didn't build a safe place,
I built a coffin.
The purpose of these fences was to lock them out,
Little did I realize,
All I accomplished was locking myself in.

# Fallen On MY Sword

How dare I reminisce
When it was my fault we parted?
I played with red flames,
So, I haven't the right to complain about my burns.

Living with myself has become an unbearable challenge.
I watched the best thing to ever happen
Walk out of my life.
I was too stubborn and ignorant to see my faults.

The same flaws that scream in my head every day.
My errors bounce off the walls
Off of my head like a never-ending echo.
I believed my lies of security.

Yet, in the end my morals need to be questioned.
And here I am, fallen on my sword.
Truly, I am the peasant responsible
For his own ill will.

# Lost Journal Entry of a Black Man #2

## (Freed Man, Year 1866)

As a black man, living in physical chains is all I know.
Waking up knowing steel shackles hang around my wrists and ankles
Is a fate I only knew to be the worst kind of living;
Yet, here I am, a freed man, still under the thumb of whites.
To them, blacks are mice caught under the paws of a starving street cat.
Freed, but what is the difference between living in physical chains, to the counterparts of mental ones?

Promised land that was never given.
Unable to vote.
Unable to find a house.
Unable to feed my family.
So, thank you for taking off the physical chains.
But these mental ones... they have to be abolished.

# Restless

We toss and turn in our beds
Trying to find any form of comfort.
The hours waste away, as our minds
Still won't drift away in sleep.
The problem is the bed we lay our heads in.
That is the easy conclusion.
What if the real problem is deep inside of us?
Buried beyond the layers of concrete
Walls we put up.
Somewhere so rarely traveled...
We never would choose to search there.
So, we toss and turn each night.
Flattening out lumps in our beds that aren't really there.
Afraid to face the music,
That the real problem is in our heads.

# Slowly Shattering

Something is definitely wrong in my head.
As these tears rush from my eyes, I'm beginning to like them.
Every drop of water from my face glides across my skin like a
masseuse.
When I don't have tears falling, I feel so empty.
I feel as if no emotions belong to me besides these darker ones.

Why do these tears feel so good down my face?
I know I'm hurting, and my eyes feel so full of pain.
I know something is wrong with me because I like the pain.
I want the pain; I need the pain.
Without pain, I won't get to enjoy the tears I hold so dear.

I think I'm breaking.
Who am I even?
I can feel myself changing.
Who am I though?
I already shattered.

## Sunken

I wish I could just sink into the ground.
I'd become a part of something bigger than myself.
I truly believe this would be a feeling better than any other.
If I could sink, everyone would soon forget me.
All my mistakes would be forgotten.
Soon enough, I would forget myself.
No longer would anxiety and depression control me.
Maybe then I would be able to sleep at night.

## Temptation

I'm poking a sleeping tiger.
I know it'll cause my destruction,
But I can't stop tripping over my own two feet.
I'm a catalyst to my own demise.
I'm a self-destruct button itching to be pushed.
Simply put, I'm mortal,
And I can't beat this monster alone.

# The Greed in Your Eyes

As I'm drowning, I wonder
How much are you going to charge me to receive your help?
How high will you drive your prices in search of getting richer?
"Quid pro quo," you tell me, as your eyes are wide hoping to drain
my wallet.

You are not human.
You are a seven-headed beast with the goal of getting richer.
And I, a mortal man, am unable to pay those high prices.
Leaving me to be trampled under the massive feet of you—
disgusting monster.

How much money did it take for you to lose your humanity?
To watch as I drown in these waters, and to care nothing of it.
You would rather I lose my life, than you lose resources to help
me.
How dare you put a price on a human's life!

I cannot hold my breath any longer.
I flail my arms in hope that your heart has even a single ounce of
compassion.
As my vision fades, I look to you once more.
As I stare into your greed filled eyes, you stare into my desperate
ones.

I can see the hunger for money in your face.
You would really rather watch me die than lend a helping hand.
The last words I hear of this wretched world come from you.
Then everything goes dark.

# Floor of the Abyss

The hours neither here nor there.
Life, an abstract painting none of us quite get.
In the darkest time, we hope to find ourselves.
If we don't, we run through life's maze again.
I hate the gray clouds and what they bring.
I hate that no day passes without them being seen.
Hours pass as I never find the answers.
Stuck hoping for someone to save me.
Will I ever bask in the light again?
The path to light promises many pains.
Hiding in darkness seems to be easier.
Although it offers no salvation.
The hours are never here nor there.
To light, I may never see again.
Cloaked in an abyss with no hope.
Stuck wondering if I'll ever be there again.

## Comfort

I fell in love with
The thought of being alone.
Sometimes I try
Just so when I fail I can
Return to my lonely state.

## The Grizzly Bear

Loneliness is a poison,
One that I drink all too much.
Unbeknownst to most,
Bears live in solidarity.
I wonder if they realize how dangerous
Closeness can be.
Solitude is deadly as well though.
The longer you're alone,
The less you care about being together
Because you would never hurt yourself
The way others do you.
In pain and confused—
I took a lesson from the Grizzlies.
Human interaction is becoming ever so unimportant.

# The Question With No Answer

Look at this grip you have on me.
Physically, my heart aches being without you.
Mentally, my thoughts want you to never leave.
Emotionally, my spirit cries out needing your love.

How could a feeling such as love be described as beautiful?
Truthfully, love might be amazing,
But with none in return, it's a darkness I cannot escape.
Love with no one to share it with is pain.
Isn't that funny, love and pain,
Two words of equal weight, yet polar opposites.

You have caused me more pain than I can handle.
All this pain has moved our relationship nowhere,
Leaving me to question myself, wondering...
If I could, would I erase the memory of you from my head?

This question splits me in two about you.
Half my mind wants to get you out of my head;
The other half not wanting to lose the only part of you that I can
control... my thoughts of you.
Erasing my memory of you would be easier, but still... it's love.

# To Kill a Rose

Why do I need a full garden?
All I want is you, my Rose.
Your beauty is more than enough for me.
So, why spoil our relationship with other flowers?

I admit, I tried to plant a daffodil without you knowing.
So intrigued with your loveliness, I tried to add a bow to a present
already perfectly wrapped.
Sadly, I was only seeing a growing garden for its appeal
And not for the pain it brings on the only flower I care for... you.

*To Kill a Rose* is no challenging feat.
I could have pulled you out of my garden in hopes of replacing
you.
Instead, I pulled the daffodil out of my garden.
Now my eyes are back to staring at you, my gorgeous Rose.

You, my elegant flower, truthfully complete me.
As feelings arise from me that no flower has ever given me,
I realize the value in a garden is not the quantity of its flowers;
It is in the quality of a lone flower.

Placing another flower next to you almost killed you.
I won't take your stunning looks for granted again.
You deserve the world my delicate, delicate flower.
But for now, give me time to gather my things, so I can at least
give you my world.

# Twice

The aftermath of our time together is pure pain.
Waking up without you is a poison I'm being forced to consume
every morning.
Sleeping has become full of the terrors of not having you,
Only to wake up and realize those terrors are real.
Every second is spent wishing the sadness would flee.
Hoping that my heart would mend over time.
Unfortunately, healing doesn't seem possible.
And the crazy thing is,
Knowing all the pain that splitting up has caused me,
Feeling so drained and lost every day.
With the depths of despair becoming my living state.
If I had the choice to relive from the beginning 'til now,
From the moment I laid eyes on you 'til now,
I would do it all over again.
Because those few moments...
Those are the moments we humans live for.
We live for the rare moments that make us truly feel alive.
You made me feel so lively.
So yes, most people would disagree with me.
But I would live through it all over again.
And I wouldn't even think twice.

# Never Satisfied

Through my fingers, life slips
Like water pouring into a cup with a hole in the bottom.
I can never have enough of what's in front of me.
Will I miss out on the achievements along the way?
One failure screams louder than a hundred successes.
As time gets up and walks away,
I sit still, frozen on past events.
My hands are the cup,
My fingers outstretched to grab more are the holes,
Life is the water falling through.
I continue to miss out.

# If Only I Could Tell You...

With a heart so heavy, I'm surprised it hasn't fallen out of me.
I hate these moments, when all I want to do is explain how I feel,
But words haven't been invented to express this shocking pain.

I feel like...

A dog that waits on the porch for his owner to return.
Unbeknownst to the dog, his owner will never walk up the steps
of the porch again.
I would give my right arm if it meant you could be here next to
me.
I'd trade fates with you if it just meant you could still be here
today.

Thank you for being you.
Thank you for being an inspiration.
Thank you for being someone I found hope in.

# Mental Blockage

If I could fly,
I would never come back.
I'd go so far away,
And because I love you so much,
My mind would still
Be with you.
I know we separated,
But I can't stop thinking about you.

# Unresolved Issues

I would say I miss you,
But you already know that.
Instead, I want you to know that I fell today.
I didn't fall physically; I fell mentally.
I started the day off so happy.
Then I realized, you aren't here.
Even worse, you chose to not be here.
Even worse, you know how sad I get when you leave.
You chose to stop trying.
Did you get tired of getting up and leaving?
Is that why you stayed gone?

# Living in Regret

It's hard to be this person,
This person from a different land.

Being without you just doesn't make sense.
For what is my heart without your hand to hold it?
That's like a rocket ship out of fuel,
Or a dress that cannot be worn.
Maybe it's a shoe that just doesn't fit,
Or perhaps it's like the sun with no moon.

I cannot stand our distance.
I hate that I caused it.

## Damaged

So afraid to die,
I lost sight of life.
So blind to love,
I don't deserve my eyes.
I'll toss them in the trash,
For fear they would
Ruin a blind man's perception of life.
For eyes that fail to see what's real
are worse than no eyes at all.

## Victory and Defeat

Yeah, I love you,
But I can't keep focusing on you.
It hurts badly,
And no, I don't know how,
But I will get past you.
You win.
You moved on, and I'm still hurting.

## Not Myself

I wonder if
I'm good enough
Or if I'll fail.
Will I keep rising
Or will I sink?
I miss the sunshine;
Too often it rains.
Sometimes, I get this way
For not being myself.

## Inner Battle

Who do I turn to
When I am my worst enemy?
Every solution I hear,
The other "me" hears it, too.

## Punishment

I'm not saying I deserve darkness,
But I sure don't deserve your light anymore.

## Live Alone

We are born alone,
Which is why I choose to live alone.
So when I die alone,
It won't be that different from living.

## Self-inflicted

I never wanted to tell you;
I just wanted it to happen.
The more I held it in,
The more I began to hurt.
That's why I could never be mad—
The pain was self-inflicted.

## Lost

I think I'm lost today.
Somehow, I lost my way.
Confused on topics I'm trying to convey.
If you were here, what would you say?

## Obviously Hidden

Should I blame you for the anger I feel?
Or is it my fault for failing to see
What was right in front of me?

## Space

I gave you space, but I always wanted
To be by your side.
Believe me, my heart was always in the right place.
Even when I wasn't physically by your side...
My heart never left yours.

# I Hate Poetry

I'm in a fight with my mind,
And I can't win.

Forced to face my darkest emotions,
Emotions that were buried so deep until this process began.

This process of repeatedly living through my greatest fears,
Fears that keep me awake at night.

Nights filled with thoughts that I cannot hope to control,
Lack of control leads to nightmares.

These nightmares that were once suppressed,
Are now more vivid than ever.

Like a tyrant, these nightmares rule the busy streets of my mind.
I'm being held against my will to relive the most painful
experiences of my life.

Who has this much power over me?
Not who, but what?

The truth is,
Poetry brought out feelings that were dormant.
Feelings I never want to express again.

So, forgive me for speaking rashly, but
I hate poetry.

# Curse

I was cursed
To have eyes hungry with desire.
A heart rate that never
Rises or falls too far.
Each success leaves only
A stronger need for the next.
Eyes so sharp and detailed,
They see the blood flowing in the prey's body.
Cursed with eyes that want more.
Doomed to never have enough.

# Cost of Sanity

You drive me away,
But I'm your only true friend.
When the tides of life flip
And love incinerates into hate,
I'll still be here—
Rooting for your success—
Even if it happens at the sickening
Cost of my sanity.

# Depths of my Heart

I need sleep,
But I can't close my eyes.
Something about being away from you
Takes the word "lonely" to another depth.

Your name echoes off the walls of my heart.
Your name is bittersweet in my mouth.
As amazing as it feels to say it,
We both know that route all too well.

I'll end up falling in love all over again.
You'll end up hurting me once more.
Like a fly in honey,
My mind will be stuck on you.

And how will I ever hope to move on?
No, I cannot say your name.
For if I do, I'll fall in love once more,
And I can't endure that anymore.

# 10-9

You were right.
I should have said it back
On that night.

I was scared
Of being in that state
Of euphoria with you.

My heart only beats for you.
I can't say 'sorry' enough.
Guilt won't let me rest.

I miss the shine in your eyes.
You brought out the best in me.
And I managed to ruin that.

I was wrong,
I was a complete fool.
I regret that day.

I loved you.
I still love you.
I will always love you.

## Lasting Memories

Wrapping my arms
Around memories so
Tightly for fear
Of them escaping.

Memories—
All I have left
Of our failed
Mission to fly together.

# I am Done

I am so done.
Figuring a way out of this hole has seemed impossible.
Trying to escape, I just kept digging.
I kept tunneling.
Of course, I couldn't free myself of this hole.

To flee is not to keep mining lower and lower.
Getting out of this hole means to stop digging for something
that's not there.
I've been trying all this time to fix my mental state.
Yet, I kept digging for a treasure that was never there.
I was going insane trying to find a prize that is not deeper.
A reward that I cannot attain by excavating.

To free myself is not to keep hope in a situation that is hopeless.
To keep fighting is not to keep drilling for nothing.
To fix my mental state, why am I still holding on
to a treasure map that leads nowhere?
A map that will only cause further confusion and pain.
To rid myself of this hole.

Looking to the future and letting go of something unattainable.
All this time I've been reaching out, grasping the air hoping it
would turn into treasure.
There is nothing for me down here.

There is no prize.
And if there is... keep it.
I'm not doing this for you anymore.
I want peace and tranquility for myself.
I'm ready to heal.

# Raven

The power behind your words far exceeds my breath.
In your eyes I find beauty;
In your heart I find home.
Although our peak has yet to come,
A peak so high you were scared to climb with me.

The height of our love scared you.
Is that why you ran off?
Was it fear of our love?
Why does light scare more than darkness?
You feared our peak
And fled like a Raven in the night.

# New Moon

Phase Four

# A Thought Unspoken

(A tribute to Langston Hughes)

What happens to a thought unspoken?
Will it forever be in my mind?
Or will it disappear like a ghost?
Does it halt like a deer in headlights?
Perhaps it evaporates like water on a hot afternoon.
Maybe it slips out the back of my head like a criminal fleeing
prison.
Are all thoughts like prisoners in our heads?
By speaking out loud, does it now become free?
Or maybe it isn't a prisoner;
Maybe it's just being held on a leash.
As time goes on, the leash gets weaker, perhaps this is how it will
escape.
Could it be that as new thoughts are pushed in,
Other thoughts are pushed out to make room?
Or will it just get up and walk away like a housewife tired of being
beaten?
In that case, why should it stay?
But, if it does leave, can I call on it again?
By not speaking aloud, does it even belong to me anymore?

After all, it is air and air belongs to no one alone.
Was I simply too scared to say it aloud?
Did I fear your answer that much?
How is it that by not saying it aloud,
regret runs rapidly throughout my head?
By holding my tongue, a fire has been set in the empty field
of dry grass I call my mind.
Speak now or forever hold your peace, and sadly,
I chose the latter.
So, what happens to this thought unspoken?
Will it ever leave and take the troubles with it?
What if I'm looking at this the wrong way?
This thought unspoken is making my life harder.
Perhaps it is not prisoner to my head.
Is it possible that this thought is holding my mind hostage?
From this perspective, how do I escape a thought unspoken?
Will I forever be prisoner and at the mercy of my mind?
Is it too late to speak the words that never left my mind?
As I sit on the floor in my mental prison,
Behind these mental walls I realize...
A thought unspoken never leaves.
Instead, it morphs into regret.

# My Digging Shovel

It was so peaceful outside when I began digging.
Every second that passed, the hole got a little deeper.
And with that, my mind became a prison for my thoughts.
A prison that hurt to live in.

Now that I'm out of the hole I dug so deep,
Looking into the hole is laughable.
Thinking about all the time I spent digging.
All of that for something that wasn't even there.

I just had a brief thought, what if I was close.
That maybe if I dug for one more day,
Perhaps even one more second,
I would have found what I was looking for.

So yes, I picked up the shovel once more,
And I threw it down the hole I was previously excavating.
As I watched my digging shovel fall into a hole I would never
return to,
I laughed and simply said,
"I'm past that phase."

# A Unyque Stranger

Sometimes I don't want a friend;
Sometimes I prefer a stranger.
Someone who won't choose to judge me
Someone who genuinely wants to help,
Rubbing shoulders with one I know nothing about...
And to receive help beyond a dollar amount.
This makes me question how many heroes in
Plain clothes I blindly pass each day—
Those with hearts so pure,
And who share words so unyque
They are blessings to be counted.

## Determined

Contrary to popular belief,
Strength is not an outer trait.
True strength is buried so deep inside of us
That only those willing to dig for it will find it.

## Rebuild

Destruction is beautiful.
How else do we rebuild?
Breaking down the old
To craft the new is amazing.
After all, each night we destroy ourselves.
While we sleep, a blueprint is laid out.
And when we awaken, we construct our new selves.

# If The Moon Could Sing

How is it that you are so much bigger than I,
Yet your personality is so small?

You were once a giant to me,
But now I see you are a mere mouse hiding behind a wall.

Projecting a shadow that made you appear to be 14 feet tall.

If the moon could sing to me, I hope it would sing me no wrong.
No longer on your feet, I guess if nobody is around to hear it, you
still do fall.

The moon told me the truth about your fears;
They are more in your head than they are in reality.

The thing you feared all along was never really there.
Look behind the curtains and you'll see.

These are the words the moon sang out to me.

# We Are the Moon

I didn't realize that I grew
Until I was presented with the
Same situation I was in years ago.
The way I reacted was poor and selfish.
So wrapped up in thinking the world revolves
Around me that my happiness fled.
I believed reality was anything my mind constructed.
Now I find, that my mind can manifest
Thoughts that may never come to fruition,
And that is okay.
Like the moon, I go through phases.
My mistake was believing that I am alone.
We all grow and see things differently in time.
We are all the moon.
Presented with the same challenge,
But this time I breathe and respond differently.
As weird as it may be,
Letting go is a useful tool.
So here I am, letting go of past mistakes.
Of burdens you nor I need to carry anymore.
Raise a glass to what lies ahead.
And may we continue to progress through our phases.

# Smile

I see it's dark and cloudy outside,
I smile.
I got fired from my job,
I smile.
I get ridiculed by other people,
I smile.
I break my arm,
I smile.
I realize my friends backstabbed me,
I smile.
I watch the love of my life walk off,
I smile.
I watch my house burn down,
I smile.
I get beat up and robbed,
I smile.
I watch my significant other get shot and killed,
I smile.
I see my son is dying from cancer,
I smile.
I know my daughter won't live past one,
I smile.
Because... if I cry about everything wrong in life, I'll cry for the rest
of my life.
There is something good in today, find it, and hold it forever.

# Powerless

There is so much power in the powerless
To be un-feared by all
Grants all the more power.
Not wielding any special blade.
Nothing unique, other than
The lack of skills that warrant defeat.
But is defeat really the problem?
Or is it the feeling of despair, knowing
You could have done more?
What is the fight if there is no other
Struggle to be pushed through?
This is the power in the powerless.
Nothing to lose, but everything to gain.

## Rain

You carry so many different views.
You are soothing to the reader.
You are gloomy to the grieving.
You are beauty to the ocean.
You are pain to the picnickers.
You are peaceful to the sleeper.
You are alarming to the adolescence.
You lead to beautiful rainbows.
You cause gross debris.
Nothing is as misunderstood as you.
In one's eye you are vicious like the Kraken.
In another, you are delicate like a dolphin.
You never change.
Yet, everyone views you differently.

# Spoken Like a Hero

Color me with peace.
There is no rain today.
Not a dark cloud in sight.
No pain is coming this way.
I felt the wrath of a nation
Fall on my name.
I did what was best for the masses,
Now, it's my name on the stake.
Oh, what a sick twist of fate.
Weight of all the world on me,
Crushing all my strength.
But yes, I would do it all again
Because the world is better for it.
Even if I'm seen as the villain,
I know I did everything I could.
Color me with your pain.
That way you hold no burdens.
Let the cloud of misery follow me each day;
That way, you will never deal with this pain.
Color me how you see fit.
Tear me down, or lift me up.

# Strength

To keep fighting,
In spite of the troubles around
Is an ability beyond my reach.
The weight of the world
Crushes my heart constantly.
Everyday a new burden.
In a cycle of constant breaking,
I still try to figure it out
How will I ever have time to rebuild?
In the faces of all my adversaries,
What events will transpire?
Will I break into pieces?
How do I stand on my own feet?
The weaker I feel,
My problems only mount.
To my surprise...
I stand taller.
Having no idea how to solve the
Many problems in front of me,
Yet, my confidence doesn't waver.

# Excavation

How many steps will it take
To find the hidden answer?
I searched all over the globe.
I dug deep and flew high,
In hopes of finding the answers we all seek.
Desperate to gain the key to happiness.
The key that one cannot purchase.
Years pass and family has come and gone.
Inching across the frozen ground,
Praying I don't fall through.
Of course, the ground caves and
The freezing water surrounds me.
Oxygen becomes low.
Light begins to dim.
Yet, the key is in my hand.
Years of searching led to this moment.
Not just any moment,
But my dying moment.
The key was always inside of me.
In fact, it's in every one of us—
Placed next to our heart is the key.

# There's Always More

No, I'm not the same anymore.
I see the forest for more than the trees now.
At times we all break down,
But in time I've learned we all can be free.
I've learned that to grow
Takes much watering from the can
Of life that grooms us each day.
Most importantly, though,
I've learned that we will hit our lowest lows.
And when we do, we stand once more.
We fight back to where we need to be.

# Tethered Forever

I know that you're changing
Because I am, too.
Even though we've grown apart,
We still are connected
By the bond of our love.
Or at least by the bond of what it was.

# Why Write?

It takes my mind off of life.
It's an escape goat
To somewhere that the
World's problems don't exist.
A place where hatred
And fear don't dictate reality.
That place is buried so deep
In my mind
That even I have trouble reaching it.
I write, not to impress others,
Only to escape this Earth.
I write with the hopes
Of finding the meaning behind
Being truly free.
Free from problems
I cannot hope to solve.
To free my mind is
Quite challenging,
But freedom is the only gift
Worth giving or seeking.

## Unseen

To be a fly on a wall
Is an amazing thing.
Being one grants the ability to listen
And learn from others' mistakes.

## Confidence

In a group belonging not to me—
Called and questioned
Like a member of the group.
But I'm red nosed and I
Stand out beyond all measures.
So, keep the scales,
I'm in a class of my own.

# The Universe of My Mind

The gift of the universe is
Beyond my reach,
So, I turn to control my mind.
Thoughts swirl and unwanted memories stick.
Control over my mind is beyond difficult.
My mind being a universe on its own.
Maybe I shouldn't try to control it.
Maybe I should just let go.

# Still Here

The sun still rises,
As it does—
I still wake.

The clock keeps ticking,
As it does—
I still grow.

The Earth continues spinning,
As it does—
I still evolve.

# Weight of Words

Words
Hold more value
Than any real
Human connection
In the end,
Human connections
May change
But words—
Words are forever.

# Rose in the River

I am a rose in the river,
Flowing the direction life chooses for me.
You are the rose in the wind,
Destined to blow to unimaginable greatness.
Once partners on the same tree,
Now strangers in this big world.
When we meet again,
Should we meet again,
I hope to rebrand myself.
See me not as the garden from which I came.
Much less should you see me as the river.
Come to know me for myself.
Whether we connect or not,
Lady fortune should decide.
All I ask is to be seen not in the
Negative light of my home,
But to be viewed by the picture
I paint when we meet again...
Should we meet again.

# Who Are We to the Stars?

I wonder if the stars look to us
With admonition in their eyes.
And as we pass by in this big blue orb,
I wonder if while we wish to the stars,
If they wish upon each of us.
I truly believe the stars
are envious of each of us.
The closeness, as humans, we have.

# Lessons From Above

What is the lesson in our stars?
They give us light in the dark,
Beauty in our routines,
Even happiness in gloominess.
Most importantly, they disappear.
Stars are here today,
May be gone tomorrow—ebb and flow.
As they come and go,
Life moves on.

## Conversation With Failure

To never fall is to never try.
I'd rather fall a thousand times
So long as I never die.
Failure is so dear to me,
That I cry when I succeed.
Truly, I miss the feeling of hating you.
Failure, come sit next to me.
But, don't you dare foreshadow what's to happen next.
Allow me to fight tooth and nail.
And if the worst should happen...
Leave me be.
For you are not to rule over me.
You, my friend, are a psychological threat meant to conquer the
mind,
but I won't let you.
So please, take the seat next to me
and let's talk about the past.
For I know I failed too many times in a row,
but this time I'll succeed.

## Time

As I grow older,
My words begin to change.
For better or worse?
Only time has the answer to that.
My words keep changing,
And my mind follows suit
As a direct result of it.

## Watering Can

I shine, not like jewelry.
I don't enhance communication like the phone.
I cannot transport you like the newest car.
I am not glamorous in any way.

So, what purpose do I serve?
I'm a rusty can whose only job is to hold water and pour it out
onto plants.
I'm not a mere gilded item.
For what I lack in glamour, I show in my worth.

# Stories to Tell

What will I say dear friend?
Should we ever meet again?
Will I cry at the joy of seeing you?
Will we talk about old times?

I hope I see you again.
We should share a laugh again.
You need to give me a call.
I hope to find you old friend.

If we ever meet again...
Oh, the stories we will have to share.
Should we ever meet again,
We will never leave again.

## Lacking Answers

I don't have all the answers—
I'm just like you,
But I'm willing to listen,
And I'm ready to learn how to be better.

## Rushed

Sometimes time is rushed.
We look to stars wondering if time moves just as fast up there.
Sometimes time is far too slow—
Like a snail that creeps across our gaze.
When really time is just independent.

# Taming the Wild

They test my mind
To know my heart.
Little do they know
A test cannot determine who I really am.
Why can't we just let a star shine?
Desperate to put a leash around it.
They'll miss the beauty of it,
Trying to tame what is better left untamed.

# Rare

We hold what's dear to us.
Each second is a snowflake
In that there will never
Be another just like it.
Should this be the last moment we share?
Let us not live as if tomorrow is our day.
Standing on our feet,
Hoping to find strength.
Yeah, we are changing,
Much like the Earth and its seasons.

# End of the Maze

I prayed for it to end.
At its peak, it was time eating.
At its valley, it was dreadful.
Sprinting through this dark tunnel,
Hoping to reach the end light.
Never, not once did I expect this.
Upon reaching the end line,
I find myself nostalgic.
Reminiscing over the tunnel.
The awful,
Beautiful,
Terrible,
Interesting,
Sickening,
Lovely tunnel.
One that I took for granted.
This journey changed me,
For better or worse has yet to be decided.
How dare I look to the past?
One that I cursed myself for choosing.
I miss the tunnel that I can no longer return to.
The finish line is nothing without the journey endured.
I was so ready for it to end.
Yet, I hate that it ended.
So, why did I pray for it to end?

# Repetition

Constantly repeating cycles
Of the good and the bad.
Mistakes made keep surfacing
As the good times leave and come.
No moment ever stays long.
No moment ever cares enough.
I wonder if this will be the last
Time I loop on this rollercoaster of life.
I believe I'm ready to exit the ride.
Tired of looping around to the same events.
Ones that bring out the worst and the best.
No longer curious of what's to come.
There is no mystery, no gamble,
No bet to be made.
We will all be back.
That's the thing about this "circle"
That we call life.
No matter where we go,
We always find a way back to the start of it all.

# Polka Dots

Clouds are like polka dots in the sky.
Beautiful blue above,
Is interrupted by the fluffy
White spaces in the sky.

Funny how this can be seen—
My life is like the big, blue sky above.
You came into my life like
Clouds do to the sky.

You grow in my life,
Like clouds grow across the sky.
Soon, the whole sky is covered
Just as my life is covered by you.

The big, blue sky is no more.
The sky, and my life, are now gray
As clouds cover from
East to West and North to South.

Sadly, my life has become gray
As you travel through my mind.
Clouds will rain down and
It will cause bad days.

Just as the clouds cause the rain,
You cause tears down my face.
But, the rain will leave,
And a rainbow shall shine.

Will my rainbow's pigment be bright?
Will my sun shine once more?
I'm sitting, hoping the pain will subside.
Patiently waiting for my sky to clear.

# Relief and Resolve

I really can't be mad.
You're the best part of my past.
I have nothing but thanks for you.
As my phases pass me by,
I'll never forget the beauty in our time together.
You brought me to my highest peaks,
And dropped me to my farthest depths.
You taught me so much, and yet I know there is more to learn
from you.
Finally, I can smile.
I'm smiling because no one can take what we had.
Dare I say, what we still have.
No, we don't talk anymore.
But I'll be damned if I ever forget you.
So, thank you, thank you so much.
Thank you for allowing me to go through my phases.

# About the Author

*Tre Hands ...*

is a Senior at Palm Beach Lakes Community High School. He is the son of Lorenzo and Tera Hands, also graduates of the Home of the Rams, as well as of The Florida State University. Tre has an older brother, Ty, who currently attends FSU.

Tre has always excelled in academics. As a result, he is a member of the National Honor Society, the Spanish Honor Society, and the National Society of High School Scholars. He is soon to be inducted in the National Technical Honor Society as well. Tre is also a member of the Biotechnology Academy, among other clubs and organizations. As a junior, he earned a Harvard Book Award. Further underscoring his stellar performance, Tre is currently the number one student in his graduating class and has been for the past three years.

As a student-athlete, Tre is a fourth year Varsity letterman for the Lakes Baseball Team. He has also played Varsity Basketball and Golf. For the school, he earned the titles "Athlete of the Year" and "Scholar Athlete of the Year" for three consecutive years.

Tre's interests are varied and have vacillated over the years— basketball, baseball, engineering, communications, business, etc. Still in an exploratory phase, he is hoping to discover his true passion and future career as he attends college. One thing has proven consistent with him and that is his love of reading and writing. This book captures one of Tre's favorite past times and hobbies; the poems within it depict his many moods at different times, as well as his relationships, friendships, and overall personality.

What many others do begrudgingly, Tre does willingly, enthusiastically, creatively, and *PASSIONATELY*!

## Credits...

Waxing Moon
www.timeanddate.com

Full Moon
www.smithsonianmag.com

Waning Moon
www.eso.org

New Moon
www.forbes.com

Keep in touch!

@theonly.trehands

Made in the USA
Middletown, DE
12 August 2022

71200498R00118